CAROL STREAM PUBLIC LIBRARY

3 1319 00472 5195

WITHDRAWN

W9-BMN-847

EDGE BOOKS

CAPTAIN

LEVEL 4

PAPER AIRPLANES

BY CHRISTOPHER L. HARBO

CAPSTONE PRESS
a capstone imprint

Carol Stream Public Library
Carol Stream, IL 60188-1634

TABLE OF

J
745.592
HAR

contents

7/11

COMMAND THE SKIES

Congratulations on making the rank of captain! You have hours of flight experience under your belt. Now the safety of your passengers and crew rests on your shoulders. The time has come to strap in and take command.

LeveL 4

As captain, you face the most challenging paper folding. Don't worry if your planes don't look perfect right away. Your first try can be a test plane. Fold the models a second time to make them perfect. Your dedication will pay off when your planes soar with serious airtime.

materials

Every paper airplane builder needs a well-stocked toolbox. The models in this book use the materials listed below. Take a minute before you begin folding to gather what you need:

 **paper**
Any paper you can fold will work. Notebook paper is always popular. But paper with cool colors and designs gives your planes style.

 **scissors**
Keep a scissors handy. Some models need a snip here or there to fly well.

 **rubber bands**
Rubber bands can send some airplane models sailing. Long, thin rubber bands work well.

 **paper clips**
Paper clips are perfect for adding weight to a plane's nose. Keep a supply of small and large paper clips on hand.

 **small binder clips**
Small binder clips also give weight to a glider's nose.

Techniques and Terms

Folding paper airplanes isn't difficult when you understand common folding techniques and terms. Review this list before folding the models in this book. Remember to refer back to this list if you get stuck on a tricky step.

VALLEY FOLDS

Valley folds are represented by a dashed line. The paper is creased along the line. The top surface of the paper is folded against itself like a book.

Mountain FOLDS

Mountain folds are represented by a pink or white dashed and dotted line. The paper is creased along the line and folded behind.

Reverse FOLDS

Reverse folds are made by opening a pocket slightly and folding the model inside itself along existing creases.

Mark folds are light folds used to make reference creases for a later step. Ideally, a mark fold will not be seen in the finished model.

Rabbit ear folds are formed by bringing two edges of a point together using existing creases. The new point is folded to one side.

Squash folds are formed by lifting one edge of a pocket and reforming it so the spine gets flattened. The existing creases become new edges.

FOLDING SYMBOLS

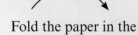
Fold the paper in the direction of the arrow.

Fold the paper behind.

Fold the paper and then unfold it.

Turn the paper over or rotate it to a new position.

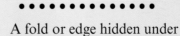
A fold or edge hidden under another layer of paper; also used to mark where to cut with a scissors

7

FIGHTER JET

Traditional model

Want a fighter jet that is always ready for its next military mission? This stylish plane swoops through the air. It's a great flier that looks super cool.

materials

* 6.5- by 11-inch (17- by 28-centimeter) paper

2 Valley fold in half.

Start Here

1 Valley fold edge to edge and unfold.

7 Valley fold the model in half and rotate.

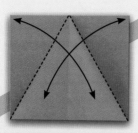

3 Valley fold the corners and unfold. Note how creases run from the center to the bottom corners.

4 Valley fold the corners to the creases made in step 3 and unfold.

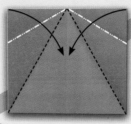

5 Squash fold using the creases made in steps 3 and 4.

6 Mountain fold on the existing creases.

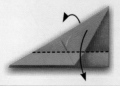

8 Valley fold the top layer. Repeat behind.

9 Valley fold the top flap of the wing. Repeat behind.

turn page

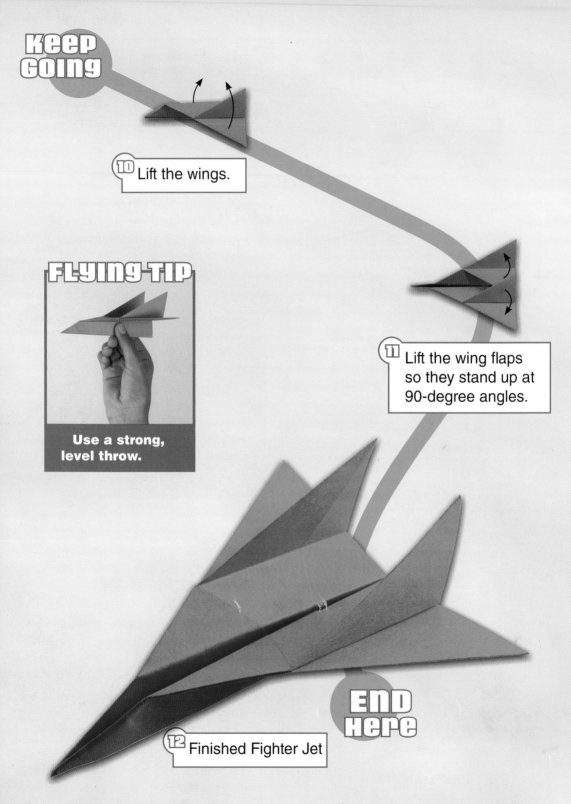

KEEP GOING

10 Lift the wings.

FLYING TIP

Use a strong, level throw.

11 Lift the wing flaps so they stand up at 90-degree angles.

END HERE

12 Finished Fighter Jet

WARTHOG

DESIGNED BY CHRISTOPHER L. HARBO

The Warthog is a beast. It may not be pretty, but this little glider soars long distances through the air. Don't worry about hitting the wall. The Warthog's snub nose can take a beating.

MATERIALS

- 8.5- by 11-inch (22- by 28-cm) paper

START HERE

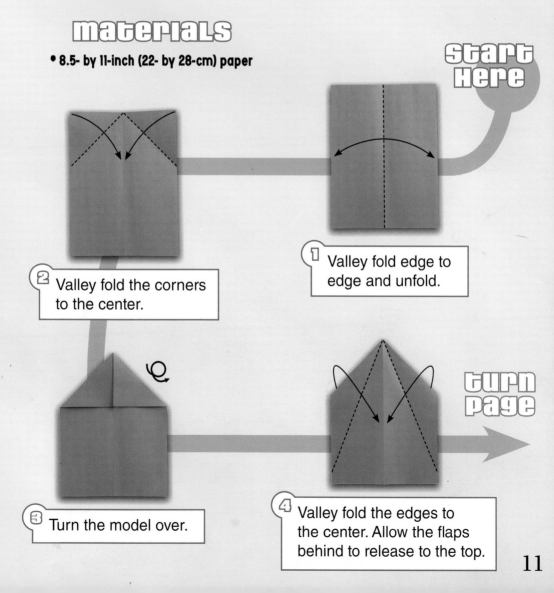

2 Valley fold the corners to the center.

1 Valley fold edge to edge and unfold.

TURN PAGE

3 Turn the model over.

4 Valley fold the edges to the center. Allow the flaps behind to release to the top.

11

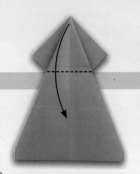

5 Turn the model over.

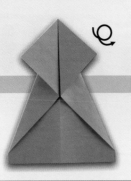

6 Valley fold the point.

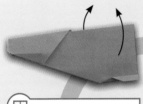

11 Lift the wings.

10 Valley fold the wing flap. Repeat behind.

12 Lift the top layer of the wing flaps and the nose flaps so they stand up at 90-degree angles.

13 Pull the wing flaps outward.

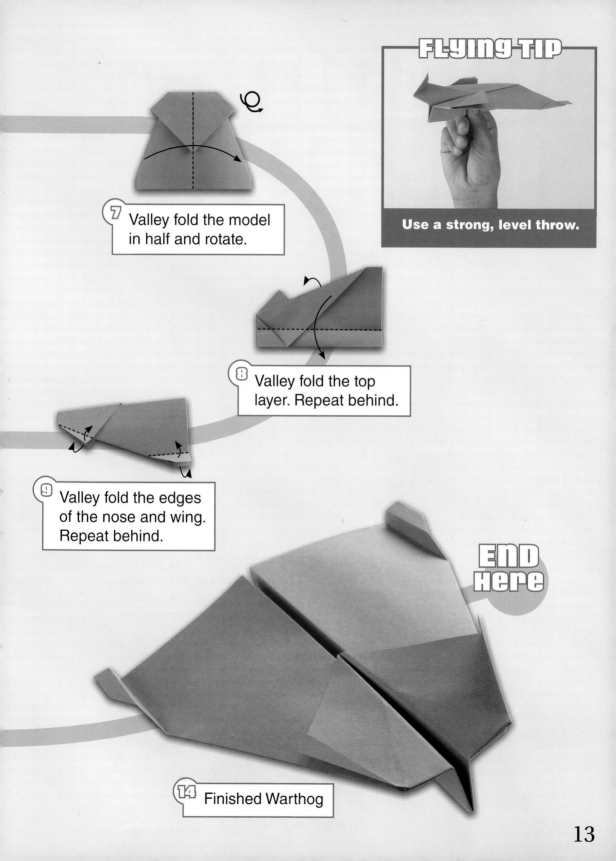

Use a strong, level throw.

7 Valley fold the model in half and rotate.

8 Valley fold the top layer. Repeat behind.

9 Valley fold the edges of the nose and wing. Repeat behind.

END Here

14 Finished Warthog

13

GLIDING Grace

DESIGNED BY CHRISTOPHER L. HARBO

Flying the Gliding Grace takes a soft touch. Throw it too hard and it goes into a steep dive. But a smooth, medium throw sends this model soaring. It's the perfect plane to practice your launching skills.

materials

* 8.5- by 11-inch (22- by 28-cm) paper

6 Valley fold to the crease made in step 2.

7 Valley fold on the crease made in step 2.

9 Valley fold the model in half and rotate.

8 Turn the model over.

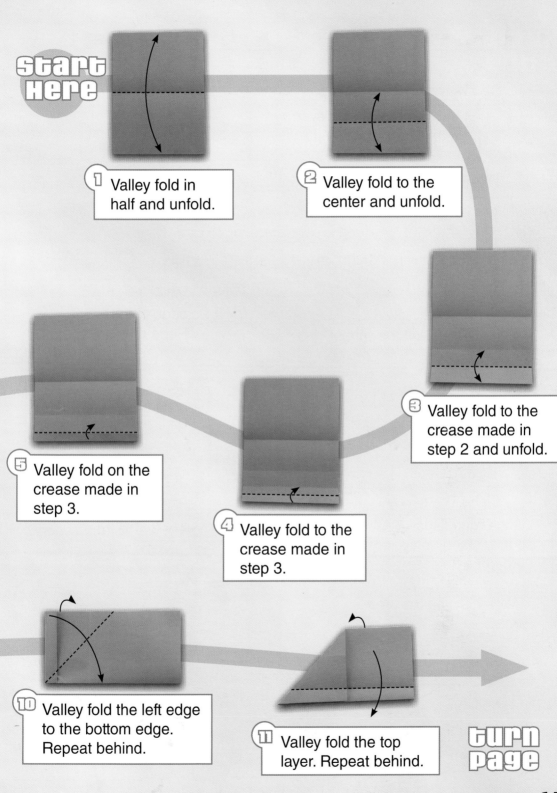

start
Here

1 Valley fold in half and unfold.

2 Valley fold to the center and unfold.

3 Valley fold to the crease made in step 2 and unfold.

4 Valley fold to the crease made in step 3.

5 Valley fold on the crease made in step 3.

10 Valley fold the left edge to the bottom edge. Repeat behind.

11 Valley fold the top layer. Repeat behind.

turn
page

15

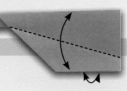

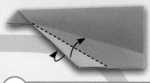

12 Valley fold the wing even with the top edge and unfold. Repeat behind.

13 Valley fold to the crease. Repeat behind.

14 Valley fold the edge of the wing. Repeat behind.

15 Lift the wings.

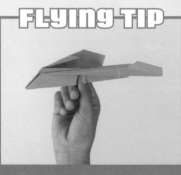

Use a soft throw with a smooth, level release.

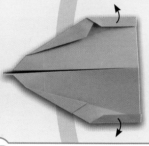

16 Lift the wing flaps so they stand up at 90-degree angles.

17 Finished Gliding Grace

FLYING ACCORDION

Can a paper plane with so many peaks and valleys really fly? Fold the Flying Accordion and find out. This unique glider will have your friends begging you to make them one.

materials

* 8.5- by 11-inch (22- by 28-cm) paper

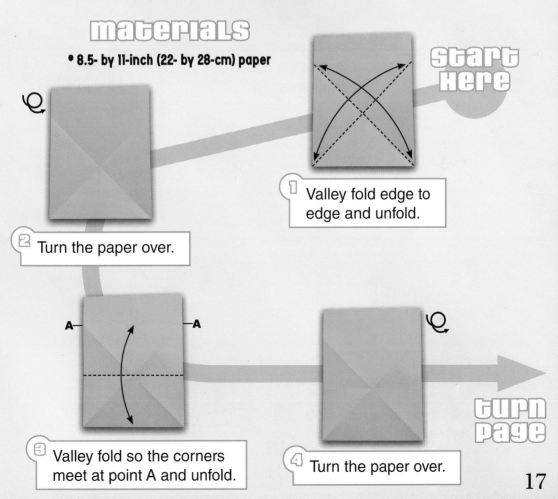

Start Here

1 Valley fold edge to edge and unfold.

2 Turn the paper over.

3 Valley fold so the corners meet at point A and unfold.

4 Turn the paper over.

turn page

17

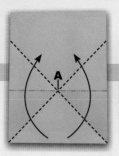

A

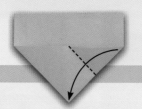

5 Push at point A. Collapse the paper on the existing creases to form a triangle.

6 Valley fold the top layer to the point.

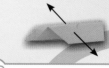

12 Mountain fold the model in half and rotate.

11 Mountain fold the point.

13 Valley fold the top layer. Repeat behind.

16 Pull out the wings.

14 Valley fold the top layer. Repeat behind.

15 Valley fold the top layer. Repeat behind.

18

7 Valley fold to the center and unfold.

8 Valley fold to the center and unfold.

9 Rabbit ear fold on the creases formed in steps 7 and 8.

10 Repeat steps 6 through 9 on the left side.

FLYING TIP

Pinch the plane on the triangle beneath its wings. Give it a medium, level throw.

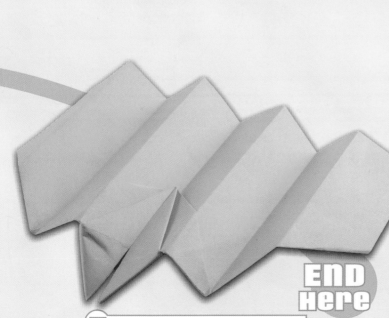

END Here

17 Finished Flying Accordion

Space BOMBER

TRADITIONAL MODEL

The Space Bomber looks like it flew in from another world. Don't let this plane's boxy shape fool you. Its flight paths are amazingly straight and long.

materials

* 8.5- by 11-inch (22- by 28-cm) paper

Start Here

1 Valley fold in both directions and unfold.

2 Turn the paper over.

A— —A

3 Valley fold so the corners meet at point A and unfold.

4 Turn the paper over.

20

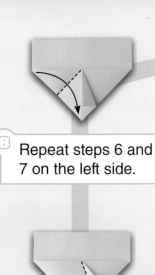

8 Repeat steps 6 and 7 on the left side.

9 Valley fold the point.

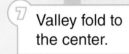

7 Valley fold to the center.

10 Unfold the two flaps beneath the point.

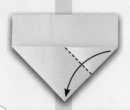

6 Valley fold the top layer to the point.

11 Tuck the flaps into the pockets of the point.

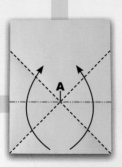

5 Push at point A. Collapse the paper on the existing creases to form a triangle.

12 Valley fold to the center.

turn page

13 Valley fold to the edge.

14 Valley fold to the edge.

FLYING TIP

Pinch the plane on the triangle beneath the wings. Give it a medium, level throw.

15 Repeat steps 12 through 14 on the left side.

16 Pull the edges of the wings out to create U-shaped channels. Turn the model over.

END
Here

17 Finished Space Bomber

Sparrowhawk

Traditional model

Do you want the Sparrowhawk to sail like a glider or loop around like a stunt plane? Changing the power and angle of your throw will determine how this plane flies. Either way, the Sparrowhawk doesn't disappoint.

materials

* 8.5- by 11-inch (22- by 28-cm) paper

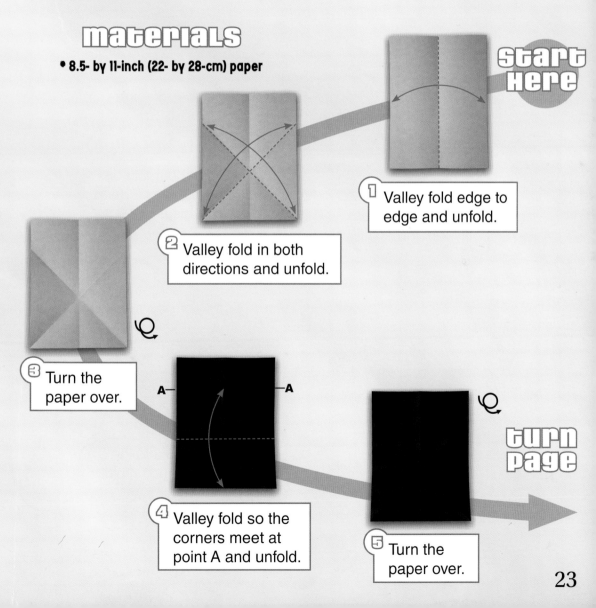

start Here

1. Valley fold edge to edge and unfold.

2. Valley fold in both directions and unfold.

3. Turn the paper over.

4. Valley fold so the corners meet at point A and unfold.

5. Turn the paper over.

turn page

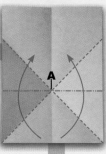

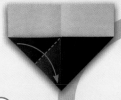

6 Push at point A. Collapse the paper on the existing creases to form a triangle.

11 Repeat steps 7 through 10 on the left side.

7 Valley fold the top layer to the point.

10 Rabbit ear fold on the creases formed in steps 8 and 9.

8 Valley fold to the center and unfold.

9 Valley fold to the center and unfold.

12 Mountain fold the point.

13 Valley fold the model in half and rotate.

18 Finished Sparrowhawk

FLYING TIP

For smooth flights, give the plane a medium, level throw. For stunt flights, give it a hard throw with a steep upward angle.

17 Lift the wing flaps so they stand up at 90-degree angles.

14 Valley fold the top layer. Repeat behind.

15 Valley fold the top layer. Repeat behind.

16 Lift the wings.

25

screech OWL

TRADITIONAL MODEL

With its wide wings and narrow tail, the Screech Owl glides like a silent hunter. Hold it as high as you can to get the longest flight.

materials

* 7- by 10.5-inch (18- by 27-cm) paper
* scissors

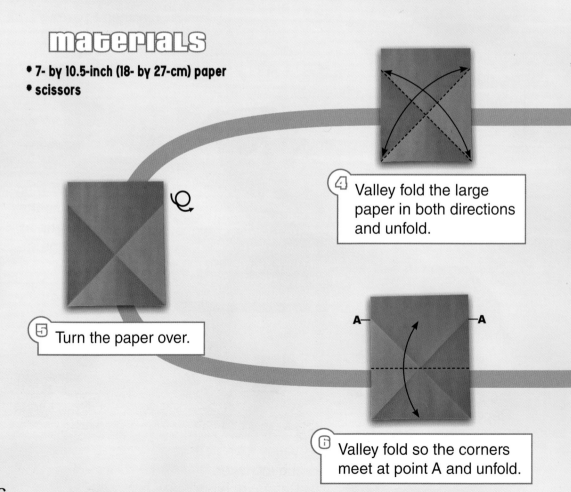

4 Valley fold the large paper in both directions and unfold.

5 Turn the paper over.

A ——— A

6 Valley fold so the corners meet at point A and unfold.

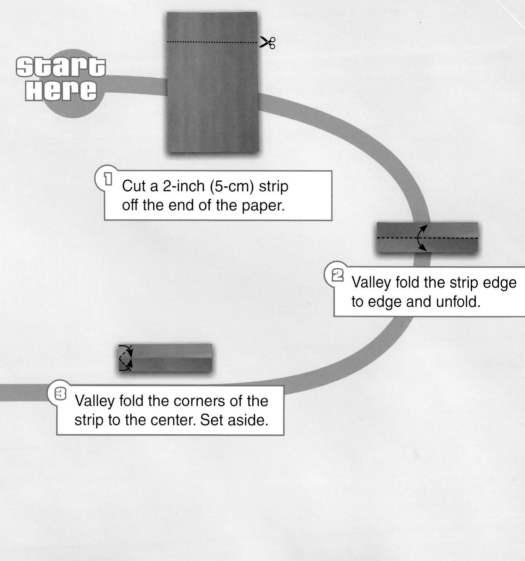

Start Here

1 Cut a 2-inch (5-cm) strip off the end of the paper.

2 Valley fold the strip edge to edge and unfold.

3 Valley fold the corners of the strip to the center. Set aside.

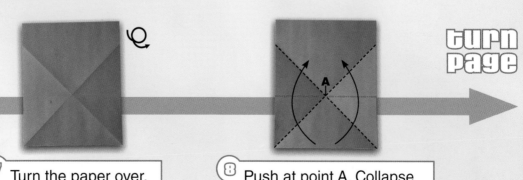

turn page

7 Turn the paper over.

8 Push at point A. Collapse the paper on the existing creases to form a triangle.

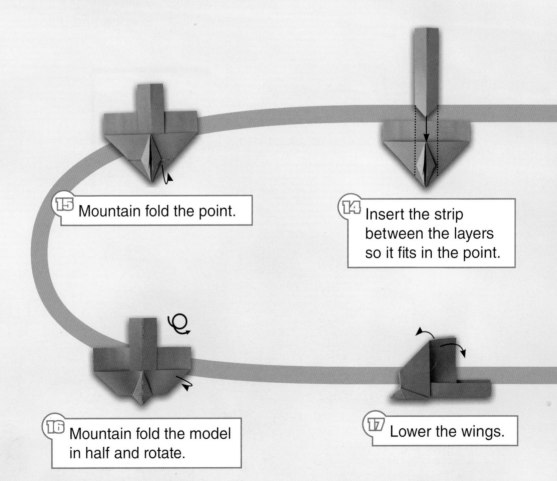

9 Valley fold the top layer to the point.

10 Valley fold to the center and unfold.

15 Mountain fold the point.

14 Insert the strip between the layers so it fits in the point.

16 Mountain fold the model in half and rotate.

17 Lower the wings.

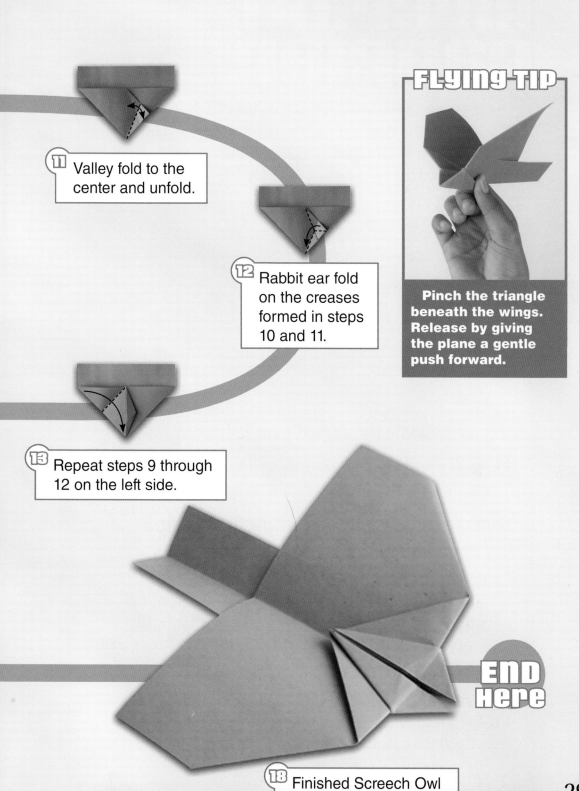

11 Valley fold to the center and unfold.

12 Rabbit ear fold on the creases formed in steps 10 and 11.

13 Repeat steps 9 through 12 on the left side.

END Here

FLYING TIP

Pinch the triangle beneath the wings. Release by giving the plane a gentle push forward.

18 Finished Screech Owl

29

Aircraft Carrier

Fighter pilots use incredible skill to land their speeding jets on aircraft carrier decks. Here's your chance to test your landing skills. Challenge a friend to a game of Aircraft Carrier.

materials

- rope
- 3 hula hoops
- 2 paper airplanes
- pencil
- notepad

What you do

1. Place a short piece of rope on the ground at one end of your yard. This rope is your throwing line.

2. Walk 10 steps from the throwing line and lay one hula hoop on the ground.

3. Walk another 10 steps and lay the second hoop on the ground.

4. Walk 10 more steps and lay the third hoop on the ground.

5. Return to the throwing line and take turns launching planes toward the hoops. Planes that land in the first hoop score 3 points. Planes that drop in the middle hoop score 5 points. Planes that land in the farthest hoop score 10 points.

6. Write down the scores of each flight on a notepad. Then add the scores for each player. The player with the highest score is the champion.

Read More

Blackburn, Ken. *The World Record Paper Airplane Book.* New York: Workman, 2006.

Dewar, Andrew. *Fun and Easy Paper Airplanes.* North Clarendon, Vt.: Tuttle Pub., 2008.

Harbo, Christopher L. *The Kids' Guide to Paper Airplanes.* Kids' Guides. Mankato, Minn.: Capstone Press, 2009.

Internet Sites

FactHound offers a safe, fun way to find Internet sites related to this book. All of the sites on FactHound have been researched by our staff.

Here's all you do:

Visit *www.facthound.com*

Type in this code: 9781429647441

Edge Books are published by Capstone Press,
151 Good Counsel Drive, P.O. Box 669, Mankato, Minnesota 56002.
www.capstonepub.com

Copyright © 2011 by Capstone Press, a Capstone imprint.
All rights reserved.
No part of this publication may be reproduced in whole or in part,
or stored in a retrieval system, or transmitted in any form or by any means,
electronic, mechanical, photocopying, recording, or otherwise, without
written permission of the publisher.
For information regarding permission, write to Capstone Press,
151 Good Counsel Drive, P.O. Box 669, Dept. R, Mankato, Minnesota 56002.
Printed in the United States of America in North Mankato, Minnesota.
032010
005740CGF10

 Books published by Capstone Press are manufactured with paper
containing at least 10 percent post-consumer waste.

Library of Congress Cataloging-in-Publication Data
Harbo, Christopher L.
  Paper airplanes, Captain level 4 / by Christopher L. Harbo.
    p. cm.—(Edge books. Paper airplanes)
  Includes bibliographical references.
  Summary: "Provides instructions and photo-illustrated diagrams for making a
    variety of traditional and original paper airplanes"—Provided by publisher.
  ISBN 978-1-4296-4744-1 (library binding)
  1. Paper airplanes—Juvenile literature. I. Title. II. Series.
  TL778.H3732 2011
  745.592—dc22   2010001003

Editorial Credits
Kyle Grenz, designer; Marcie Spence, media researcher; Marcy Morin, scheduler;
  Laura Manthe, production specialist

Photo Credits
Capstone Studio/Karon Dubke, all planes and steps
Shutterstock/newphotoservice, cover (background); Serg64, cover (background)